Harry Swotter

A Harry Potter

Quiz Book

Rich Jepson

UNOFFICIAL & UNAUTHORISED

Quiz Books by Rich Jepson

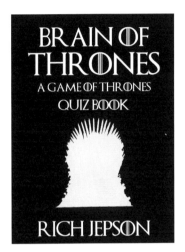

Harry Swotter – A Harry Potter Quiz Book

Disclaimer: All questions within this book were sourced from reliable, reputable sources. If you find any questions, which you, the reader, believe are incorrect, then please contact the publisher directly so amendments can be made.

Acknowledgements

Unauthorized and unofficial, this book is not endorsed by anyone associated with either the Fantastic Beasts or Harry Potter films, books or video games. It is purely a fun, friendly trivia book designed to test the knowledge of fans of the series.

Introduction

In 1990, J.K. Rowling was travelling from Manchester to London's King's Cross station when her train became delayed. She passed the time by devising a story about a young boy who discovered he was a wizard.

Fast-forward a few decades and that young wizard has become one of the most iconic characters in literary and cinematic history.

The Harry Potter book series has sold over 450million copies worldwide, receiving numerous awards and accolades along the way. These historic novels have charmed the hearts of millions of fans of all ages across the globe and it's from these books that the Harry Potter film series was spawned – and that's where this book comes in.

Inside *Harry Swotter,* you will find 25 quizzes consisting of 15 questions each, questions become increasingly difficult as you advance through the book. There are 15 general knowledge rounds and 10 rounds based on specific subjects or themes, including a quiz on *Fantastic Beasts and Where to Find Them.*

There's also a round of tiebreakers designed to help you figure out who really knows the most about Harry Potter. That's 385 questions covering everything there is to know about J.K. Rowling's Wizarding World.

Harry Swotter is a fun, friendly quiz book designed for fans of the Harry Potter film series to enjoy. Whether you're using it for a pub quiz, testing your friends and family or flying solo…

Good luck, have fun and keep quizzing.

Contents

QUESTIONS

QUIZ 1 - General Knowledge

1   Which actor plays Harry Potter?

2   Where does Hagrid take Harry to buy his school supplies?

3   What is the name of Harry's owl?

4   What shape does Harry's Patronus take?

5   Where in their house did the Dursleys make Harry sleep when he was a child?

6   What platform is used for the Hogwarts Express?

7   What is the name of Harry's cousin?

8   What was Harry's first broomstick?

9   What is the name of the wizarding world's newspaper?

10 Where does the Dursley family live?

11 Which schoolhouse is Harry sorted into?

12 Who teaches potions at Hogwarts?

13 What shape is Harry's scar?

14 What object is Professor Slughorn disguised as when Harry first meets him?

15 Who is the 'Prisoner of Azkaban'?

Answers - Page 68

QUIZ 2 - General Knowledge

1   Where do Harry and Cho share their first kiss?

2   What creatures guard Azkaban?

3   What is the name of Dumbledore's phoenix?

4   What was the name of Ron's pet rat?

5   What did the Boggart turn into when Parvati Patil faced it?

6   What nickname is used for civilians outside of the wizarding world?

7   Who is the caretaker at Hogwarts?

8   How did the Dursleys explain the death of Harry's parents to him?

9   What is the name of Fred and George's joke shop?

10 What is the name of the journalist who interviews Harry during the Triwizard Tournament?

11 Which character does Emma Watson play?

12 What are Hagrid's students told they must do when approaching a Hippogriff?

13 How many decoys of Harry are made to deceive Voldemort and his forces?

14 Who is the 'Half-Blood Prince'?

15 How do members of the wizarding community send their mail?

Answers - Page 69

QUIZ 3 - General Knowledge

1   What is the name of the portrait that guards the entrance to Gryffindor Tower?

2   What vehicle picks up Harry at the start of the *Prisoner of Azkaban*?

3   What initials does Harry find written on a piece of paper inside the fake locket?

4   What does Hagrid do to Dudley during his first visit to the Dursleys?

5   What subject does Professor McGonagall teach?

6   Which character does Rupert Grint play?

7   What object does Draco Malfoy first try to send through the vanishing cabinet?

8   What is the name of Hermione's cat?

9   What is the name of the network that wizards use to travel between fireplaces?

10 What was the name of the Hagrid's three-headed dog?

11 How many Weasley children are there?

12 What object does Hermione use in order to attend multiple classes at the same time?

13 What was the name of the House-elf who served the House of Black?

14 What colour is the Slytherin coat of arms?

15 Who discovers Harry injured, beneath his invisibility cloak, on the Hogwarts Express?

Answers - Page 70

QUIZ 4 - General Knowledge

1 Who is Harry's godfather?

2 What false name does Harry give the staff of the Knight Bus?

3 Who was Hermione's date for the Yule Ball?

4 What type of blood dripped from the ceiling inside the house Horace Slughorn was staying in?

5 What does Lupin give to Harry to make him feel better after the dementor attack on the Hogwarts Express?

6 How many years have passed between the battle of Hogwarts and the final scene of *Deathly Hallows Part 2*?

7 Who is the charms teacher at Hogwarts?

8 Which chess piece did Ron replace in the chessboard chamber?

9 Which character died whilst Harry was being transported from Privet Drive to The Burrow?

10 What's the name of the Hippogriff that injures Malfoy during the care of magical creatures class?

11 Where did Harry's parents live?

12 Where do Harry and Ginny hide the Half-Blood Prince's potions book?

13 Who was the first person to get sorted into a Hogwarts house?

14 Which actor plays Professor Severus Snape?

15 Who bought Hedwig for Harry?

Answers - Page 71

QUIZ 5 - General Knowledge

1 Who finds the Room of Requirement for Dumbledore's Army?

2 Which actor plays Rubeus Hagrid?

3 How old is Harry when he finds out that he is a wizard?

4 Whose memory shows a young Tom Riddle at his orphanage?

5 Who built the Chamber of Secrets?

6 What does Bellatrix insist that Snape make with Narcissa Malfoy?

7 What is the name of Hagrid's Acromantula, which Harry and Ron encounter in the Forbidden Forest?

8 What item did Harry receive from Dumbledore in his will?

9 Who sent Harry a Firebolt broomstick in *The Prisoner of Azkaban*?

10 Who told Umbridge how to enter the Room of Requirement?

11 Where is the Slytherin common room located?

12 What type of dragon does Harry fight in the first task of the Triwizard Tournament?

13 What flavour of 'Bertie Bott's Every Flavour Bean' did Dumbledore unfortunately eat when he was young?

14 What does Sirius mistakenly call Harry shortly before he is killed?

15 What does Harry want to be after he graduates from Hogwarts?

Answers - Page 72

QUIZ 6 – School Houses

Which schoolhouse did the following characters belong to?

1   Luna Lovegood

2   Tom Riddle

3   Moaning Myrtle

4   Cedric Diggory

5   Gregory Goyle

6   Padma Patil

7   Parvati Patil

8   Zach Smith

9   Sirius Black

10 Severus Snape

11 Seamus Finnigan

12 Justin Finch-Fletchley

13 Regulus Black

14 Ginny Weasley

15 Cho Chang

Answers - Page 73

QUIZ 7 - Quidditch

1　How many players are there on each Quidditch team?

2　How many points does a team receive for a goal?

3　What are the 3 kinds of balls used in Quidditch?

4　How many goal hoops does a keeper defend?

5　What shape are Quidditch pitches typically?

6　Who won the Quidditch World Cup in *The Goblet of Fire*?

7　Which team does Gwenog Jones represent?

8　How many points does a team receive for catching the golden snitch?

9　What position does Darco Malfoy play?

10　Which country did Viktor Krum play Quidditch professionally for?

11 How long is a Quidditch pitch?

12 Which Quidditch position does Ron play?

13 Who is the Hogwarts Quidditch referee and flying teacher?

14 What is the name of the broom the Slytherin team all ride in *The Chamber of Secrets*?

15 Who is the Gryffindor team captain when Harry joins the team?

Answers - Page 74

QUIZ 8 – He Who Must Not Be Named

1 Which city was the orphanage where Voldemort grew up in?

2 What is Voldemort's real name?

3 What are the members of Voldemort's army called?

4 What subject did Voldemort want to teach at Hogwarts?

5 Which Hogwarts Professor came to the orphanage to tell Voldemort he was a wizard?

6 Which house was Voldemort in at Hogwarts?

7 Who did Voldemort blame for opening the Chamber of Secrets?

8 What was Voldemort's blood status?

9 Who helped restore Voldemort to his body?

10 Who was Voldemort's favourite teacher at school?

11 Who was killed when the Chamber of Secrets was first opened?

12 What does Voldemort take from Dumbledore's tomb?

13 Where does Voldemort say Harry must give himself up in *Deathly Hallows Part 2*?

14 Which actor played Lord Voldemort in Harry's first year?

15 What was Voldemort's mother called?

Answers - Page 75

QUIZ 9 – Patronus

Can you identify the animal form of each character's patronus?

1   Ron Weasley

2   Ginny Weasley

3   James Potter

4   Albus Dumbledore

5   Cho Chang

6   Hermione Granger

7   Seamus Finnigan

8   Minerva McGonagall

9   Severus Snape

10 Arthur Weasley

11 Dolores Umbridge

12 Luna Lovegood

13 Kingsley Shacklebolt

14 Remus Lupin

15 Aberforth Dumbledore

Answers - Page 76

QUIZ 10 – Fantastic Beasts and Where to Find Them

1   Which year is the film set in?

2   What is Newt Scamander's occupation?

3   What is the American word for muggle?

4   What is the name of the wizarding speakeasy Newt visits?

5   What does MACUS stand for?

6   Inside what department store does Newt Scamander find the oversized Occamy?

7   What creature helps Tina Goldstein escape death?

8   What are Occamy eggs made out of?

9   What kind of factory does Jacob Kowalski work in?

10 What is the name of Newt's Thunderbird?

11 Which house was Newt part of at Hogwarts?

12 Who directed the film?

13 What is the name of the creature that attempted to rob the Steen National Bank?

14 What is the New Salam Philanthropic Society (NSPS) otherwise known as?

15 What kind of dessert does Queenie make for Jacob and Newt?

Answers - Page 77

QUIZ 11 - General Knowledge

1   Who is the Beauxbatons Academy's school champion?

2   What is the name of the pub where the three friends go for a Butterbeer?

3   What creature can Rita Skeeter turn into?

4   How do Harry and the others escape Gringotts after they take a Horcrux?

5   Which sweetshop does Harry invisibly enter in *the Prisoner of Azkaban*?

6   What sentence does Umbridge instruct Harry to write with a 'blood quill'?

7   Who gives Harry the Gillyweed for the second Triwizard challenge?

8   Which actress plays Minerva McGonagall?

9   What is the Diadem of Ravenclaw?

10 Who does Harry take to the Yule Ball?

11 What is the new motto for the Ministry of Magic after it is taken over by Voldemort's forces?

12 Which 3 objects make up the Deathly Hallows?

13 Who helps Harry figure out what to do with the golden egg?

14 Who sets fire to The Burrow?

15 Which schoolhouse has a badger on its coat of arms?

Answers - Page 78

QUIZ 12 - General Knowledge

1 How do you open 'The Monster Book of Monsters'?

2 What does Harry use in the Headmaster's office to see Snape's memories?

3 What breed is Hagrid's pet Dragon?

4 What does Ron receive from his mother after she finds out he and Harry drove the flying car to Hogwarts?

5 Which school house's coat of arms is blue in colour?

6 Why does Harry fall off his broomstick in the Quidditch game against Hufflepuff?

7 What word does Bellatrix Lestrange carve into Hermione's arm?

8 What item did Ron receive in Dumbledore's will?

9 Which actor provides the voice of Dobby?

10 Who disguised himself as 'Mad Eye' Moody in *The Goblet of Fire*?

11 What is the name of the map that shows every person's location within Hogwarts?

12 Which chess piece did Harry replace in the chessboard chamber?

13 Which character does Gary Oldman play?

14 Who supplied Harry with his first wand?

15 Who did Neville Longbottom take to the Yule Ball?

Answers - Page 79

QUIZ 13 - General Knowledge

1   Which actor plays Professor Filius Flitwick?

2   Who leads Harry, Ron and Hermione through the passageway to Hogwarts, shown to them by Aberforth?

3   What is the name of the Squib who witnesses the demontors attack on Harry and Dudley?

4   Which sweets created by the Weasley twins cause instant 'sickness'?

5   Where did the Snatchers take Harry, Ron and Hermione?

6   Who did Ron turn into when he and the others snuck into the Ministry of Magic?

7   What potion is used to create the Harry decoys?

8   Who is the House Ghost of Hufflepuff?

9   Who is the person that Ron beats to become Keeper for the Gryffindor Quidditch team?

10 What was the name of the student group set up by Dolores Umbridge to maintain order in Hogwarts?

11 When Bellatrix and Narcissa Malfoy visit Snape, before the start of school term, who do they find living with him?

12 What colour are Dobby's eyes?

13 Where does the tunnel under the Whomping Willow lead to?

14 What did the Boggart turn into while facing Professor Lupin?

15 What did Ron use to destroy Slytherin's locket?

Answers - Page 80

QUIZ 14 - General Knowledge

1   What is the common name of the potion 'Felix Felicis'?

2   What was the name of the book Hermione received in Dumbledore's will?

3   Who owns the flying motorcycle that Hagrid borrows to transport Harry to the Dursley house?

4   How far back in time does Tom Riddle's diary take Harry?

5   Who put Harry's name in the Goblet of Fire?

6   What does Harry give to Dobby to free him from his master?

7   Who serves drinks at Slughorn's party?

8   Where does Harry go when he uses the Marauder's Map for the first time?

9   Who takes over as Minister for Magic after the Death Eaters' coup?

10 What is Tonks first name?

11 Who is Sirius Black's father?

12 Who did Hermione take to Slughorn's Christmas party?

13 Who was the Hogwarts Professor of Muggle Studies?

14 Which actor plays Argus Filch?

15 What do Hermione's parents do for a living?

Answers - Page 81

QUIZ 15 - General Knowledge

1   What does OWL stand for?

2   Who does Harry take to Slughorn's Christmas party?

3   What spell is used to save Hermione from the troll?

4   What is Cedric Diggory's father's first name?

5   After escaping the wedding, which street do Harry, Ron and Hermione reappear on?

6   Who does Harry meet during his first visit to the Leaky Cauldron?

7   Who does Harry ask to help him break into Bellatrix Lestrange's vault at Gringotts bank?

8   What is the name of Hagrid's 16ft tall half-brother?

9   Which spell conjures up 'The Dark Mark' in the air?

10 What organization did Hermione start in her 4th year?

11 Whilst in Bellatrix's vault, what does Harry discover the Horcrux is?

12 Which actress plays Luna Lovegood?

13 What's the first potion Harry brews perfectly thanks to the Half-Blood Prince's instructions?

14 What is the name of the French Wizarding school?

15 When is Harry's birthday?

Answers - Page 82

QUIZ 16 – Cast and crew

1   Who directed the first two Harry Potter films?

2   Which actor went on to become the 10th Doctor in the BBC sci-fi drama *Doctor Who*?

3   Which actor played Arthur Kipps in the horror film, *The Woman in Black*?

4   Which two real-life twins played the roles of Fred & George Weasley?

5   Which Harry Potter actor also had a lead role in the *Twilight* series of films?

6   Which actress went on to star in *The Perks of Being a Wallflower* & *My Week with Marilyn*?

7   How old was actor Daniel Radcliffe when he began filming as Harry Potter?

8   Which actor also appeared in *The Patriot, Black Hawk Down* & *Peter Pan*?

9   What was the name of Alan Rickman's character in *Die Hard*?

10   How many Harry Potter films did David Yates direct?

11 Which Harry Potter actor also appeared in the BBC comedy *Life's Too Short*?

12 When auditioning, which young Harry Potter actor submitted a tape showing them performing a rap they wrote for the role?

13 Which actress went on to play Violet Crawley in *Downton Abbey*?

14 Which city was Emma Watson born in?

15 Which actor played the role of Valentin Zukovsky in two James Bond films?

Answers - Page 83

QUIZ 17 – Spells

What do each of the following spells and charms do?

1   Lumos (LOO-mos)

2   Oculus Reparo (ok-ul-lus re-pa-ro)

3   Alohomora (al-LOH-ha-MOHR-ah)

4   Riddikulus (rih-dih-KUL-lus)

5   Stupefy (STOO-puh-fye)

6   Sectumsempra (sec-tum-SEMP-rah)

7   Accio (AK-ee-oh)

8   Expecto Patronum (ecks-PECK-toh pah-TROH-numb)

9   Petrificus Totalus (pe-TRI-fi-cus to-TAH-lus)

10 Expelliarmus (ex-PELL-ee-ARE-muss)

11 Crucio (KROO-shea-oh)

12 Imperio (im-PEER-ee-oh)

13 Obliviate (oh-BLI-vee-ate)

14 Avada Kedavra (ah-VAH-dah keh-DAV-rah)

15 Wingardium Leviosa (win-GAR-dee-um lev-ee-OH-sa)

Answers - Page 84

QUIZ 18 – Deaths

Can you name the person that was responsible for the death of each of the following characters?

1   Cedric Diggory

2   Sirius Black

3   Albus Dumbledore

4   Alastor Moody

5   Nagini

6   Lily & James Potter

7   Moaning Myrtle

8   Bathilda Bagshot

9   Dobby

10 Barty Crouch Snr

11 Bellatrix Lestrange

12 Severus Snape

13 Serpent of Slytherin

14 Scabior

15 Helena Ravenclaw

Answers - Page 85

QUIZ 19 – Who said it?

Name the character that said each of the following quotes?

1   "Yer a wizard Harry"

2   "This boy will be famous. There won't be a child in our world who doesn't know his name."

3   "Come to me, let me rip you."

4   "Wit beyond measure is a man's greatest treasure."

5   "Odd sort of place, this, isn't it?"

6   "Do take care, won't you Harry?"

7   "We had to use Neville instead!"

8   "Wow, we're identical!"

9   "Oh no you don't, laddie!"

10 "And here comes Mr. Krum!"

11 "We've all got both light and darkness inside us. What matters is the part we choose to act on. That's who we really are."

12 "We are only as strong as we are united, as weak as we are divided."

13 "Greatness inspires envy; envy engenders spite; spite spawns lies."

14 "It is the quality of one's convictions that determines success, not the number of followers."

15 "Kill the spare"

Answers - Page 86

QUIZ 20 – Anagrams

Solve each of the following anagrams to reveal the name of a character

1   I BRUSHED A RUG

2   OLD BULB MEASURED

3   PEN VERSUS SEA

4   MOVING TO TELL NOBLE

5   A LOGO UNLOVED

6   A SKI CLUB SIR

7   UNSURE LIMP

8   GAMING CAVEMAN ROLL

9   TROPHY RATER

10 OLD FOAMY CAR

11 THICK GALLERY DOOR

12 EMERGING HERO RAN

13 GREAT EXTERNAL BILLS

14 MOD REVOLT

15 ONES LAWYER

Answers - Page 87

QUIZ 21 - General Knowledge

1   Who was the Quidditch commentator in Harry's first year at Hogwarts?

2   Which creatures attack Harry and Dumbledore as they try to retrieve the locket?

3   Which spell does Draco Malfoy use on Harry when he's hiding in the luggage rack?

4   Which character is also known as Moony?

5   What was the name of the female elf Dobby liked?

6   When the snatchers catch the trio, what does Hermione say her name is?

7   What exam were the fifth year students taking when Fred and George disrupted it with a fireworks show?

8   Which actress plays Ginny Weasley?

9   What object do the students have to change their animals into, during a lesson in Transfiguration?

10 What does R.A.B. stand for?

11 Who puts the love potion in the chocolates that Ron eats?

12 Which chess piece did Hermione replace in the chessboard chamber?

13 What breed of dragon did Fleur Delacour have to face during the Triwizard Tournament?

14 Which spell does Professor McGonagall cast to bring the suits of armour to life in order to protect the school?

15 Which 4 characters appear through the resurrection stone for Harry?

Answers - Page 88

QUIZ 22 - General Knowledge

1 Which bridge is destroyed by Death Eaters at the start of *The Half Blood Prince*?

2 What happened to Neville's parents that resulted in them being unable to remember their son?

3 What is the name of the goblin that gets incinerated by the Ukrainian Ironbelly?

4 Where was the lost Diadem of Ravenclaw?

5 What potion did Harry take in order to get Slughorn's memories?

6 What time do Harry and Hermione travel back to in order to save Sirius and Buckbeak?

7 Who informed Harry, Ron and Hermione of the bequests left to them in Dumbledore's will?

8 How are the Death Eaters Amycus and Alecto Carrow related?

9 Which character does Emma Thompson play?

10 What subject does Harry study in private with Professor Snape in order to help him block out his nightmares?

11 What is the main use of a Mandrake?

12 What shop on Knockturn Alley specialises in antiques related to the Dark Arts?

13 Where did Dobby transport Harry and the others to during their escape from Malfoy Manor?

14 What item did Griphook hold in his hand as he died?

15 What is the name of the Centaur who saves Harry from Voldemort in the Forbidden Forest?

Answers - Page 89

QUIZ 23 - General Knowledge

1 How did Harry survive underwater in the Triwizard Tournament?

2 Which character does Mark Williams play?

3 Who nearly dies after touching a cursed necklace?

4 How many presents did Dudley originally get on his birthday before screaming for more?

5 What is the name of Marjorie Dursley's dog?

6 Where is the Order of the Phoenix headquarters located?

7 What is the name of the Scandinavian wizarding school?

8 How much did Harry's wand cost?

9 Who took Fleur Delacour to the Yule Ball?

10 What is the name of the Executioner appointed by the Ministry of Magic to dispose of Buckbeak?

11 What is Professor Dumbledore's full name?

12 What is the make and model of the Weasley's flying car?

13 What magazine does Luna's father publish?

14 What phrase does the golden snitch reveal, after Harry presses it to his lips?

15 Who does Ron Weasley kiss in the Ministry of Magic?

Answers - Page 90

QUIZ 24 - General Knowledge

1 Who is the Conductor of the Knight Bus?

2 Which creatures attack Fleur Delacour in the second task
   of the Triwizard Tournament?

3 Who sends Harry his letter of expulsion from Hogwarts?

4 What school did the Dursley's say they sent Harry to?

5 What colour is the feather of Rita Skeeter's quill when she
   interviews Harry?

6 Who is the headmaster of the Durmstrang Institute?

7 What does Harry give Ron as an antidote after he drinks
   the poisoned mead?

8 How many murders was Sirius wrongly imprisoned for?

9 What is Harry's youngest son's name?

10 What was written on Dobby's tombstone?

11 Which actor plays Draco Malfoy?

12 What colour frosting is on Harry's birthday cake from Hagrid?

13 What's the name of James Potter's animagus stag?

14 What spell did Harry perform on Draco Malfoy during their fight in the bathroom?

15 Who wrote an obituary for Dumbledore in the Daily Prophet?

Answers - Page 91

QUIZ 25 - General Knowledge

1 Who was the Care of Magical Creatures Professor before Hagrid?

2 Who does Hermione take a hair from for the Polyjuice Potion, which accidentally turned out to be a cat hair?

3 What is Gilderoy Lockhart's favorite colour?

4 What is Nearly Headless Nick's real name?

5 What is at the core of Lucius Malfoy's wand?

6 What is the English translation of the Hogwarts motto?

7 What is the name of the fish Lily Potter gave Professor Slughorn when she was a student?

8 Which actor plays Neville Longbottom?

9 What page does Snape ask them to turn to while covering for Lupin's class?

10 What does Professor Vector teach?

11 What is the name of the landlady of the Three Broomsticks pub?

12 Where does Dudley Dursley attend school?

13 What plant did Neville Longbottom get for his birthday?

14 Who was headmaster of Hogwarts when Tom Riddle was at school?

15 What is the last word Harry speaks in the entire film series?

Answers - Page 92

TIEBREAKERS

Score tied? Whoever has the closest answer to one of the following questions wins the quiz.

1   How much, in British pounds, did the first Harry Potter film take?

2   How much, in US dollars, did it cost to create the Wizarding World of Harry Potter theme park in Florida?

3   How many copies were there of the initial print run for Harry Potter and the Philosopher's Stone?

4   How many Ford Anglias were destroyed to create the Whomping Willow crash scene?

5   How many different products are there in the Weasleys' Wizard Wheezes Shop?

6   How many times was Harry Potter's famous scar applied by the make up team throughout the whole series?

7   How many copies of *Harry Potter and The Deathly Hallows* were sold on the first day of sales?

8   How long would it take to watch the entire series of films back-to-back?

9   How many languages (to date) have the Harry Potter books been published in?

10 How much was the average earnings of each Harry Potter film, in US dollars?

Answers - Page 93

ANSWERS

Quiz 1 - Answers

1   Daniel Radcliffe

2   Diagon Alley

3   Hedwig

4   A stag

5   In the cupboard under the stairs

6   9 3/4

7   Dudley

8   Nimbus 2000

9   The Daily Prophet

10 4 Privet Drive

11 Gryffindor

12 Professor Snape

13 Lightning Bolt

14 An armchair

15 Sirius Black

Quiz 2 - Answers

1 In the Room of Requirement

2 Dementors

3 Fawkes

4 Scabbers

5 A snake

6 Muggles

7 Argus Filch

8 They said his parents died in a car crash

9 Weasleys' Wizard Wheezes

10 Rita Skeeter

11 Hermione Grainger

12 Bow

13 6

14 Severus Snape

15 By Owl

Quiz 3 - Answers

1   The Fat Lady

2   The Knight Bus

3   R.A.B

4   He gives him a pig's tail

5   Transfiguration

6   Ron Weasley

7   An apple

8   Crookshanks

9   The Floo Network

10 Fluffy

11 7

12 A time turner

13 Kreacher

14 Green

15 Luna Lovegood

Quiz 4 - Answers

1 Sirius Black

2 Neville Longbottom

3 Viktor Krum

4 Dragon's blood

5 Chocolate

6 19 years

7 Professor Filius Flitwick

8 A knight

9 Alastor "Mad Eye" Moody

10 Buckbeak

11 Godric's Hollow

12 The Room of Requirement

13 Hermione Granger

14 Alan Rickman

15 Rubeus Hagrid

Quiz 5 - Answers

1 Neville Longbottom

2 Robbie Coltrane

3 11

4 Albus Dumbledore

5 Salazar Slytherin

6 The Unbreakable Vow

7 Aragog

8 A golden snitch

9 Sirius Black

10 Cho

11 In the dungeons, under the lake

12 Hungarian Horntail

13 Vomit

14 James

15 An Auror

Quiz 6 - Answers

1 Ravenclaw

2 Slytherin

3 Ravenclaw

4 Hufflepuff

5 Slytherin

6 Ravenclaw

7 Gryffindor

8 Hufflepuff

9 Gryffindor

10 Slytherin

11 Gryffindor

12 Hufflepuff

13 Slytherin

14 Gryffindor

15 Ravenclaw

Quiz 7 - Answers

1   7

2   10 points

3   Quaffle, Bludger & Golden Snitch

4   3

5   Oval

6   Ireland

7   Holyhead Harpies

8   150 points

9   Seeker

10 Bulgaria

11 500ft

12 Keeper

13 Rolanda Hooch

14 Nimbus 2001

15 Oliver Wood

Quiz 8 - Answers

1 London

2 Tom Marvolo Riddle

3 Death Eaters

4 Defence Against the Dark Arts

5 Dumbledore

6 Slytherin

7 Hagrid

8 Half Blood

9 Peter Pettigrew

10 Professor Horace Slughorn

11 Moaning Myrtle Warren

12 The Elder Wand

13 The Forbidden Forest

14 Richard Bremmer

15 Merope Riddle (née Gaunt)

Quiz 9 - Answers

1 Jack Russell Terrier

2 Horse

3 Stag

4 Phoenix

5 Swan

6 Otter

7 Fox

8 Tabby Cat

9 Doe

10 Weasel

11 Persian Cat

12 Hare

13 Lynx

14 Wolf

15 Goat

Quiz 10 - Answers

1   1926

2   Magizoologist

3   No-Maj

4   The Blind Pig

5   Magical Congress of the United States of America

6   Macy's

7   Swooping Evil

8   Silver

9   Canning

10 Frank

11 Hufflepuff

12 David Yates

13 Niffler

14 Second Salamers

15 A Strudel

Quiz 11 - Answers

1   Fleur Delacour

2   The Three Broomsticks

3   A beetle

4   On the back of a dragon

5   Honeydukes

6   "I must not tell lies"

7   Neville Longbottom

8   Maggie Smith

9   A tiara

10 Parvati Patil

11 Magic is Might

12 The Elder Wand, the Resurrection Stone and the Cloak of Invisibility

13 Cedric Diggory

14 Bellatrix Lestrange

15 Hufflepuff

Quiz 12 - Answers

1 You stroke it down the spine

2 Pensieve

3 Norwegian Ridgeback

4 A howler

5 Ravenclaw

6 Because he sees a hoard of Dementors

7 Mudblood

8 His deluminator

9 Toby Jones

10 Barty Crouch, Jr.

11 Marauder's Map

12 A bishop

13 Sirius Black

14 Garrick Ollivander

15 Ginny Weasley

Quiz 13 - Answers

1   Warwick Davis

2   Neville Longbottom

3   Mrs Frigg

4   Puking Pastilles

5   Malfoy Manor

6   Reginald Cattermole

7   Polyjuice

8   Fat Friar

9   Cormac McLaggen

10 The Inquisitorial Squad

11 Peter Pettigrew (Wormtail)

12 Green

13 The Shrieking Shack

14 A full moon

15 The Sword of Gryffindor

Quiz 14 - Answers

1   Liquid Luck

2   The Tales of Beedle the Bard

3   Sirius Black

4   50 years

5   Barty Crouch Jr. (disguised as Alastor Moody)

6   A sock

7   Neville Longbottom

8   Hogsmeade

9   Pius Thicknesse

10 Nymphadora

11 Orion Black

12 Cormac McLaggen

13 Charity Burbage

14 David Bradley

15 They are both dentists

Quiz 15 - Answers

1   Ordinary Wizarding Level

2   Luna Lovegood

3   Wingardium Leviosa

4   Amos

5   Tottenham Court Road

6   Professor Quirrel

7   Griphook

8   Grawp

9   Morsmordre

10   Society for the Promotion of Elfish Welfare (SPEW)

11   Helga Hufflepuff's cup

12   Evanna Lynch

13   The Draught of Living Death

14   Beauxbatons Academy of Magic

15   31st July (the same as J.K. Rowling)

Quiz 16 - Answers

1   Chris Columbus

2   David Tennant

3   Daniel Radcliffe

4   James & Oliver Phelps

5   Robert Pattinson

6   Emma Watson

7   11

8   Jason Isaacs

9   Hans Gruber

10 4

11 Warwick Davis

12 Rupert Grint

13 Maggie Smith

14 Paris, France

15 Robbie Coltrane

Quiz 17 - Answers

1   Turns the tip of the wand into a torch

2   Repairs eyeglasses

3   Used to open and unlock doors

4   Transforms Boggarts into something silly

5   Stuns victim

6   Creates large, blood-oozing gashes on the subject

7   Summons an object to the caster

8   Conjures a protective spirit-like incarnation

9   Temporarily binds the victim's body

10 Causes whatever the victim is holding to fly away

11 Inflicts intense pain on the recipient of the curse

12 Places the subject in a dream-like state, in which he or she is utterly subject to the will of the caster

13 Used to hide a memory of a particular event

14 Causes instant death to the victim

15 Levitates, moves and manipulates the target

Quiz 18 - Answers

1   Peter Pettigrew (as per Lord Voldemort's orders)

2   Bellatrix Lestrange

3   Severus Snape (secretly under Albus' orders)

4   Lord Voldemort

5   Neville Longbottom

6   Lord Voldemort

7   Salazar Slytherin's Basilisk

8   Nagini

9   Bellatrix Lestrange

10 Barty Crouch Jr (posing as Alastor Moody)

11 Molly Weasley

12 Nagini

13 Harry Potter

14 Neville Longbottom

15 Bloody Baron

Quiz 19 - Answers

1 Rubeus Hagrid

2 Professor McGonagall

3 The Basilisk

4 Luna Lovegood

5 Gilderoy Lockhart

6 Molly Weasley

7 Oliver Wood

8 Fred and George Weasley

9 Mad Eye Moody

10 Mr. Bagman

11 Sirius Black

12 Albus Dumbledore

13 Tom Riddle

14 Remus Lupin

15 Lord Voldemort

Quiz 20 - Answers

1   Rubeus Hagrid

2   Albus Dumbledore

3   Severus Snape

4   Neville Longbottom

5   Luna Lovegood

6   Sirius Black

7   Remus Lupin

8   Minerva McGonagall

9   Harry Potter

10 Draco Malfoy

11 Gilderoy Lockhart

12 Hermione Granger

13 Bellatrix Lestrange

14 Voldemort

15 Ron Weasley

Quiz 21 - Answers

1   Lee Jordan

2   Inferi

3   Petrificus Totalus

4   Remus Lupin

5   Winky

6   Penelope Clearwater

7   Potions

8   Bonnie Wright

9   Water goblets

10 Regulus Arcturus Black

11 Romilda Vane

12 Rook/Castle (Queen-side)

13 Common Welsh Green

14 Piertotum Locomotor

15 James Potter, Lily Potter, Sirius Black & Remus Lupin

Quiz 22 - Answers

1 Millennium Bridge

2 The Cruciatus Curse was used on them

3 Bogrod

4 In the Room of Requirement

5 Felix Felicis

6 7.30pm (3 hours prior)

7 Rufus Scrimgeour

8 Siblings

9 Professor Sybil Trelawney

10 Occlumency

11 To restore those who have been Petrified

12 Borgin and Burkes

13 Shell Cottage

14 Godric Gryffindor's Sword

15 Firenze

Quiz 23 - Answers

1   Gillyweed

2   Arthur Weasley

3   Katie Bell

4   36

5   Ripper

6   12 Grimmauld Place, London

7   Durmstrang Institute

8   7 galleons

9   Roger Davies

10 MacNair

11 Professor Albus Percival Wulfric Brian Dumbledore

12 Ford Anglia (105E Deluxe)

13 The Quibbler

14 "I open at the close"

15 Mary Cattermole

QUIZ 24 - Answers

1 Stan Shunpike

2 Grindylow

3 Mafalda Hopkirk

4 St. Brutus' Secure Centre for Incurably Criminal Boys

5 Green

6 Igor Karkaroff

7 A Bezoar

8 13

9 Albus Severus Potter

10 "Here Lies Dobby, A Free Elf"

11 Tom Fellon

12 Pink (with green writing)

13 Prongs

14 Sectumsempra spell

15 Elphias Doge

Quiz 25 - Answers

1　Professor Kettleburn

2　Millicent Bulstrode

3　Lilac

4　Sir Nicholas de Mimsy-Porpington

5　Dragon Heartstring

6　"Never Tickle a Sleeping Dragon"

7　Francis

8　Matthew Lewis

9　394

10　Arithmancy

11　Madame Rosmerta

12　Smeltings Academy

13　Mimbulus Mimbletonia

14　Armando Dippit

15　"Ready?"

TIEBREAKER ANSWERS

1   £604million

2   $200million

3   1000

4   14

5   120

6   5,800

7   11million

8   19.6hours

9   79

10 $963,268,497